MW00981967

SPUR-OF-THE-MOMENT
GAMES
AND
LEARNING
ACTIVITIES

Mary J. Davis

ACCENT PUBLICATIONS
Colorado Springs, Colorado

Accent Publications
4050 Lee Vance View
P.O. Box 36640
Colorado Springs, Colorado 80936

Library of Congress Catalog Card Number 96-84990
ISBN 0-89636-328-7

CONTENTS

Dedication

To my husband, Larry,
and our three grown children,
Lori, Jeff, and Wendi.

I would also like to dedicate this book to church leaders
who carry a heavy load in making the church function and
grow for the glory of God. Especially to Bill, B.A., Sonny, Guy
and Jean Chase, Oscar and Nadean Davids.

INTRODUCTION

If you are a volunteer in the children's department of a church, you've faced those times when you need an extra activity to help keep children interested and actively involved in learning.

It is for these situations that this book is written. *Spur-of-the-Moment Games and Learning Activities* give you the tools you need to keep children in grades 2-6 interested. You do not have to round up extra materials. These games and learning activities are designed to give you spur-of-the-moment flexibility and creativity without extra work.

Many of them require no additional materials. Read through the book so you will have in mind things that can be used with different lessons. Needed supplies are noted with each activity.

And if your church cannot provide all of these items, encourage your parents to get involved and contribute one item from each family. Or, organize a cookie bake and use the money from that to purchase them. Put a notice in the church bulletin asking for these specific supplies. Ask your youth group to donate, help organize the cupboard, and be your classroom helpers. Be creative. Your children and your church will benefit.

Extra minutes of classroom time can be creatively used to enhance lessons and encourage Christian living. This book will help you do just that. Ideas for everything from instant games to service projects for your students will keep your classroom time interesting and fun, while teaching Christlike concepts.

Do you have a cupboard in your classroom or close by? Keep these 23 items in your resource closet, and you will be able to provide your students with instant activities that are fun and meaningful. Several of these items are the same as those suggested for *Spur-of-the-Moment Crafts* if you need to combine supplies into one resource closet. Enjoy these ideas, as you make them part of your weekly teaching of God's Word.

Paper - any kind, scrap paper will work for many of the activities
Paper bags
Newsprint rolls (or inexpensive white table covering or freezer wrap paper)
Paper plates
Old magazines
Yarn/String
Balloons
Straws
Old teaching materials
Tape recorder/player
1 or more favorite tapes of Christian music
Blank tapes
Blindfold (Oversized handkerchief, dish towel, piece of fabric)
Trash bags
Bibles
Concordance
Glue
Scissors
Crayons
Pencils
Chalkboard/chalk or Whiteboard/markers
Stapler/staples
Tape

JUST FOR FUN — INSTANT ICE-BREAKER GAMES

1. Rings Around

Students form two circles, one inside the other, both with an even number of students. If you have an odd number of students, choose one student to be caller. If you have an even number, the teacher or helper will call.

Circles begin to move, one clockwise and the other counter-clockwise. Caller turns his/her back to group. After a short time, caller says "STOP." Each student turns to the one closest to him in the other circle, shakes hands, and introduces self, giving one item of personal information. "My name is Jeff. Glad you're here. My favorite season is_____." (*This personal information could be favorite color, favorite sport, favorite class at school, favorite food, etc.*)

Repeat several times.

THINGS YOU'LL NEED...

❑ None

2. Switch

Students stand in a circle but turn to face the back of person beside them. Give two or three students a wad of paper. Instruct them to pass the paper as quickly as possible but listen to your instructions.

For example, teacher shouts, "Over the right shoulder—pass." Students pass the object only over their right shoulders. They continue doing that until the next command is given. For instance, shout faster, slower, reverse, etc. Also, change the way paper is passed: Under legs, under left arm, over head.

THINGS YOU'LL NEED...

❑ Three wads of paper

❑ One wad of paper

3. Color Pass

Students form a circle and begin passing a wad of paper. Teacher shouts out a color, and only those wearing that color can touch the paper. Paper may have to be thrown past several players at times.

Alternatives: Those whose names begin with B; anyone who brought his Bible, etc.

❑ None

4. Spin and Command

Students stand in a circle. IT stands in middle. Two students spin IT. IT holds his arms out in front of him, hands clasped. When he stops spinning, he calls out the name of the person he is pointing at with his outstretched arms. IT tells that person to do something, such as: Cluck like a chicken. Spell his name backward. This person then becomes IT.

❑ None

5. Make Room

IT stands inside circle of students. Then, she suddenly gets between two members of the circle. These two must run in opposite directions around the outside of the circle back to original spot. Last one back becomes IT.

❑ Ball of yarn
❑ One or more balloons

6. Circle Volleyball

Mark off a large circle on the floor with yarn. (You may want to tape it to the floor.) Students stand inside the yarn circle. Blow up a balloon and tie it. Use it as a volleyball. Students must not to step outside circle, while keeping balloon from touching the ground. If they do, they drop out of the circle. Continue until only one is inside the circle or set a time limit.

Alternative: Reverse the procedure by having students toss the balloon, keeping it off the floor, while not stepping inside the circle.

7. Follow the Leader Mix-Up

Students form two lines and stand at opposite ends of the room. First person of one line walks to the other line, acting out something—*e.g. Hop on one foot, walk like an elephant, pat head and rub stomach, scissors walk.*

Then, first person of other line does the same action, except going backward to the other line. *e.g. Hop backward on one foot until he gets to the other line, walk like an elephant backward to the other line, rub head and pat stomach, scissors walk backward.* When everyone has had a turn, start with opposite team, so everyone has had a turn in making up the action and in going backward.

8. Quick Catch Game

Students divide into two lines and stand at opposite ends of room. They may wish to stand a little closer when game begins. Everyone takes off one shoe and uses it as a "catcher's mitt."

Then, give each person on one side a piece of paper to wad up. Paper wad will be launched and caught by students in the other line in the shoes they are holding. **Each person throws to the person directly across from him.** If there is an odd number of students, teacher or helper should participate.

Students who catch the paper wad immediately throw it back to the person directly across from them on the other side who try to catch it in their shoes. Continue doing this as quickly as possible until only one person is still catching the paper wad.

9. Silly Story

Students sit in a line or circle. One person begins by saying one word of a made-up story.

Next student repeats that word and makes up one beginning with the last letter of the first word, and so on, for as long a time as you have.

Example: Mo**m m**ad**e e**ver**y y**ello**w w**oodpecke**r rea**d **D**an's **s**choo**l **literatur**e.**

THINGS YOU'LL NEED...

❏ Paper for each student

10. Make and Fly

A quick and fun game. Have students form a line. Give each a piece of paper. Allow two minutes to fold the paper into an airplane. Then, let them soar their planes across the room. They may retrieve their planes and try again, if time allows.

THINGS YOU'LL NEED...

❏ None

11. Goofy Introductions

Students stand up one at a time and tell something about themselves. They should say three things, and one should be exaggerated or totally false. Other students guess which statement is not true. Even if they already know each other, this game is usually fun and lively.

THINGS YOU'LL NEED...

❏ Several pieces scrap paper
❏ A paper bag
❏ Four crayons (different colors)

12. Instant Board Game

Drop pieces of paper randomly around the room. Place four crayons in a paper bag. Tell the students that each color represents a different number. *(Example: Red is one; blue is two; brown is three, and purple is four.)*

Students each take a turn reaching into bag and taking out one crayon. They then advance that many spaces around the room by stepping on the pieces of paper. They must stay on the papers, but may go any direction. Several students may land on one paper at the same time. Each must keep at least part of their foot on the paper. Object is to keep moving around the spaces until game is over.

Set a time limit on the game or play for whatever remaining minutes of class are left.

13. Funny Competition

Divide into two teams. One at a time, each team sends a comedian to the opposite team to try to make them laugh. The comedian can tell jokes, make faces, funny noises, or just laugh. (Team must be quiet when their teammate is trying to make other team laugh.)

Teacher counts off thirty seconds. If no one on that team has laughed, the comedian joins their team. At end of time, see which team has the most members.

THINGS YOU'LL NEED...

❑ None

14. Circle Around Relay

Divide into two or more teams. The first person in line walks or runs backward or sideways around their team, then sits down in the front of the line. The next person does the same until all members have circled the team.

HINT: Have teams keep hands on their laps, so fingers won't get stepped on.

THINGS YOU'LL NEED...

❑ None

15. It's a Match

Divide into two teams. Each team will have a scorekeeper. (You may have them use the chalkboard or paper, whichever is easier.) When a team is "up," one person says a word. Team members must yell objects that match. *For example:* HORSE—bridle, saddle, hay, rodeo, tail, cowboy, etc. Scorekeeper gives one point for each match. Then, other team is up.

Alternative: You will need a timer for this (kitchen timer or the second hand on a watch). Teacher chooses the words to be matched. Don't count words, but team must continue shouting matching words for thirty seconds. Other team listens for words that do not match.

THINGS YOU'LL NEED...

❑ Chalkboard
❑ Chalk
❑ Eraser
   or
❑ Paper and pencil for each team
❑ Timer, optional

16. Confusing Race

Set up a goal line at one end of the room. Line students up along a starting point. To race, they must listen to your instructions and try to reach the goal following those instructions. For instance: Teacher shouts, "Run, stop, jump, stop, come back, stop, turn around, stop, hop on one foot, stop," etc. Keep them turning toward and away from the goal several times to keep it exciting.

17. Instant Targets

Half of students are designated as targets. They assume one of the following positions: Clasp hands in front, forming a basket with arms. Clasp hands over head to form a hoop with arms. Stand with legs apart to make a wicket. Put hands on hips, forming two hoops.

Balloons, paper plates, or wads of paper are tossed through the targets. After a few minutes, students change places.

Alternative: Make the game more lively by allowing the targets to move. However, they must keep their position, hands on hips, etc.

18. Moving Basketball

Team #1 holds hands to form a circle. This team is the basket. Team #2 has several balloons, paper plates, or paper wads. They must stand behind a piece of yarn on the floor and try to get their "ball" into the "basket." Basket may move within a designated area, raise arms above heads, etc., but they must hold hands at all times.

Team #2 may not cross the line to retrieve a ball that didn't make it into the basket. However, any ball that accidentally comes back across the line may be thrown again. After a few minutes, let Team #2 count their "basket" points. Teams then switch places.

19. Heads Up Volleyball

Students kneel in a circle. Volleyball is a large trash bag filled with air. (Swish it in the air and close quickly. Tie with yarn.) Students try to keep volleyball in the air using only their heads.

THINGS YOU'LL NEED...

❑ One large plastic trash bag
❑ A piece of yarn

20. Plate Balance

Each team chooses an IT. IT stands 10-15 feet away from her team. Teacher gives each team 10 paper plates. On GO, one team member runs forward and places a plate on IT's head. Second member does the same and so on. If plates fall off, team members stop running until IT gets the plates balanced again.

THINGS YOU'LL NEED...

❑ Ten paper plates for each team

21. Nest Head

Do the same relay as above. However, IT puts a plate on his head. Each team member runs forward, wads the paper up, and places it into the "nest" (as eggs in a nest). After placing paper into nest, team members stay by IT to help him pick up nest if it falls.

THINGS YOU'LL NEED...

❑ One paper plate for each team
❑ Several paper wads for each team

22. Slide Relay

Divide into two or more teams. Each team gets two pieces of scrap paper. On GO, first member of each team slides across the floor with his feet on the two pieces of paper. He must go to the goal and back without letting his feet leave the paper. If either foot slides off the paper, he must pick it up and go back to start over. Next member uses the papers to slide to goal and back and so on, until every team member has gone.

THINGS YOU'LL NEED...

❑ Two pieces scrap paper for each team

2 INSTANT TEAM GAMES

- ❑ Nine chairs
- ❑ Colored construction paper (optional)

23. Human Tic-Tac-Toe

Arrange nine empty chairs into a tic-tac-toe square. Form two teams. Ask the students questions from the day's lesson. Each correct answer allows that team to place a student on the "board." Any completed line (vertical, horizontal, or diagonal) wins the game.

You may want to have students wear pieces of colored construction paper to designate their team as the Blue Team or Red Team.

- ❑ Nine chairs
- ❑ Chalkboard
- ❑ Chalk
- ❑ Eraser

24. Double Puzzle

Arrange nine chairs into a tic-tac-toe square. Form two teams.

Teacher thinks up a word or short phrase to correspond with the lesson. *(Examples: Red Sea, Elijah, miracle.)* She places a blank on the chalkboard for each letter of the word or phrase.

Each team guesses a letter. If the letter fits into the puzzle, the teacher places it in the appropriate blank on the chalkboard and that team gets to place a person on the tic-tac-toe square.

Play until someone wins the tic-tac-toe. Then, have the teams try to guess the word or phrase. If you keep score, teams get a point for winning the tic-tac-toe game and a point for each puzzle they solve.

25. Word Play

❑ Chalkboard
❑ Two pieces of chalk
❑ Erasers

Teacher writes on the board several words from the current lesson: *(e.g.) Sin, jealousy, tongue, kindness, soldier, battle, march, sword, etc.)* Teams then have one person write their answers for them. On GO, teams shout to their "writer" a phrase, with at least one word starting with the same letter as original word.

Examples: Stomp out sin. Jump away from jealousy. Tame the tongue. Keep showing kindness.

Writer writes the phrases down. Teacher allows a short time for the game. Then say, STOP. See which team came up with the most phrases using the key word. If time allows, have a member of each team read the phrases aloud.

26. String Out Words

❑ Ball of yarn or string for each team

Each of two or more teams is told the same word from the lesson or memory verse. Give each team a ball of yarn or string.

On GO, teams spell out the word with yarn/string. Letters must be at least one foot high. Use the floor or a long table. Have students tape the yarn in strategic places in order to maintain the shape of the letters. Word must be readable when they are finished.

Alternative: Write out a whole verse. Give each team a ball of yarn/string.

27. Human Letters

❑ None

Divide into teams of five or more students. On GO, each team spells out a predetermined word. They spell by lying on the floor and using their bodies to form the letters. Each letter may take more than one person. First team to complete the word wins.

❑ Paper wad for each
student

28. Remembering Battle

Two teams stand on opposite sides of the room. Teacher asks a question regarding the lesson or theme to a member of one team. If student answers correctly, he gets to throw a paper wad toward the other team. Then ask a question of the other team. If they are correct, they throw a paper wad back across the room. Proceed down the line of each team until every member has been asked a question. At end of game, count to see how many paper wads landed within two feet of the other team. Team with least number of paper wads wins.

❑ None

29. Side-Step

Divide into two teams. Team members stand side-by-side with arms linked. A question is asked of first team member. Rest of team is not allowed to respond. However, the opposite team can shout out wrong answers to try to get that person confused. If person gives a wrong answer, opposite team side-steps two steps toward other side of room. If person answers correctly, his team gets to side-step one step.

❑ Chalkboard
❑ Chalk for each team
❑ Eraser

30. Verse Relay

On GO, one member from each team runs to the board and writes first word of memory verse. He runs to back of line and next person runs to write second word. Keep going until complete verse is written. (This relay can be played with two or more teams, depending on how big your chalkboard is.)

❑ None

31. Inchworm

Divide class into two or more teams. Members of each team stand in a line with hands on waist of person in front. Teams start at same place, and goal is on other side of the room.

Ask question to first person in line on one team. Correct answer allows entire team to inch forward one step. Ask a question of next team and so on. First team to reach goal, wins.

32. Mixed-Up Verse

THINGS YOU'LL NEED...

❏ Paper for each student
❏ Pencils

Each member of the team gets a piece of scrap paper. Pass a pencil down the line. Each team member writes one word of the verse (or two or more words, depending on length of verse.) Then each team member crumples up the paper and tosses it into a pile about halfway across room. (One pile for each team.)

On GO, team rushes to the pile, and each member picks up a crumpled paper. Teams uncrumple papers and put verse together. Have them stand in the order of the verse.

33. How Many Words?

THINGS YOU'LL NEED...

❏ Chalkboard
❏ Chalk
❏ Erasers
    or
❏ Paper
❏ Pencils

Divide into two or more teams. Each team chooses one member to write on the board. (Or, give each team one piece of paper and a pencil.) Teacher writes a word or phrase on the board where all teams can see. *(e.g. Tabernacle, Pharaoh, Mount Sinai, Gethsemane, Lamb of God, etc.)* Team members try to make as many words as possible from that main word or phrase.

The writer writes down all the words his team members come up with. Give teams five minutes or less, depending on length of the main word.

34. Turnaround Quiz

THINGS YOU'LL NEED...

❏ Paper and pencil to keep score

Form two teams. One member of Team #1 asks the other team a question about the lesson. The other team gets a point for correct answer. Team #1 gets a point if the answer is wrong.

Then, first person on Team #2 asks a question for Team #1 to try to answer.

35. Mixed-Up Wisdom

Divide class into two or three teams. When a team is up, they stand by the chalkboard and choose a Proverb, either half or all of a verse. They must tell the class what chapter this verse is in. A writer writes the verse on the board with no spaces in between the words. Other teams have their Bibles open in order to find and guess which verse is on the board.

36. Bits of Wisdom

Divide class into two or three teams. When a team is up, they choose a Proverb and write one word on the board. They tell the class what chapter to look in. Other teams try to guess which verse, just by the one word on board. If they cannot guess, writer puts one more word on board, etc., until one of the other teams guesses which verse. (Don't write the words in order.)

To keep score, the team that guesses correctly gets a point. Or, you might assign different point values based on how many words of the verse are on the board when the team guesses which verse it is.

Depending on length of verse, 1-2 words of the verse might be worth 10 points; 3-5 words might be worth 5 points; more than 5 words is worth 1 point.

37. Shape Game

Divide class into two teams and appoint a "writer." Teacher names a shape. The writer for each team draws the shape on the board. (Make it large.) On GO, teams tell their writer things that have something to do with that shape. Writer writes the words inside the shape. After one minute, teacher calls "STOP." Count to see which team has the most words inside the shape.

Shape Suggestions: Ark, church, heart, cross, boat, stone tablets, rainbow, tree.

38. Chalkboard Crossword

THINGS YOU'LL NEED...

❏ Chalkboard
❏ Chalk
❏ Erasers

Divide into two teams. Choose a category for the entire game: Old Testament events, New Testament women, animals, foods, etc. First team writes a word on the board. Second team thinks of a word, based on one of the letters of first word. Words must relate to the category. Words can go vertical or horizontal. Game continues until one team cannot make another word. See example.

```
              A     H
        J E R I C H O
        O   K       R
        S           N
        S H O U T
        U
      W A L L S
              I S R A E L
              X       R
              D       M
          R A H A B   Y
      P       Y
    T R U M P E T S
      I
      E
      S
    C I T Y
      S
```

39. Hold onto the Word

THINGS YOU'LL NEED...

❏ Straws
❏ A slip of paper for each team
❏ Pencils

The teacher gives each team a small slip of paper and a pencil. The team writes a key word from the lesson on the paper *(e.g. Love, patience, salvation).*

Give each person on the team a straw. Set up a "goal line" on the opposite side of the room. Teams race to the goal and back to give the "word" to next team member. Race by sucking on the straw to hold the "word" paper. Team members pass the paper to the next person without using hands. Next person must take the paper by sucking on it with his straw.

Alternative: Give each person on the team a straw and a piece of paper and pencil. Have each one write a word on the paper and run to the goal as soon as the previous person is back. Each person must hold on to his paper by sucking on it with the straw. If students drop the paper, they must start over again at their team line.

40. Build a Bridge Game

Divide into two teams. Cut several straws into different lengths and put into a paper bag.

The teacher asks teams a question. The first team to answer correctly draws a straw from the bag. (Have them choose a straw quickly, so they won't have time to feel for longest straws.)

Teams keep the straws until the game is over. Then, teams line their straws along the floor to see which team can build the longest "Bridge."

41. Cooperation Relay

Divide class into pairs. Run a race with two or three pairs at a time.

Give each pair a length of yarn and 1/3 of a straw. On GO, pairs lace straw onto yarn; each person puts one end of yarn between teeth and together the pair carries the straw to a goal. They must keep the yarn taut so that the straw does not touch anyone's mouth.

42. Working Together Relay

Divide class into pairs. Pairs sit back to back with arms linked together. On GO, pairs stand up and walk to a goal, keeping arms linked.

Alternative: Divide class into pairs and form two teams of pairs. First team whose pairs all reach the goal wins.

INSTANT INDOOR GAMES

43. Rings Around the Memory Verse

Students form two circles, one inside the other, both with an even number of students. If you have an odd number of students, choose one student to be caller. If you have an even number, the teacher or helper will call.

Circles begin to move, one clockwise and the other counter-clockwise. Caller turns his/her back to group. After a short time, caller says "STOP." When circles stop, student standing in front of caller on outside circle says first half of memory verse, and other student opposite that one on the inside circle finishes.

Alternative: **Blessings.** Students tell each other three blessings in their lives or things they are thankful for when the circles stop.

Alternative: **Lesson reminder.** Inside circle says name of one character (object, city, animal) in today's lesson. Outside circle tells what they learned about that person in the lesson.

THINGS YOU'LL NEED...

❑ None

44. Listen and Rush

Have students form a circle. Give each a piece of paper to wad up and throw inside circle. Have the students back up three large steps, staying in a circle. Remove one piece of paper.

Review the lesson story, instructing the students to listen for a certain word. (Whatever word you choose.) When they hear the word, they rush to get a paper wad. The one without paper will then continue with the story. You may change the word each time a new storyteller takes over.

THINGS YOU'LL NEED...

❑ One piece of scrap paper for each student to wad

❑ One piece scrap paper, wadded

45. Creation or Noah Game

Students stand in a circle. IT stands in center. She tosses a wadded paper to someone and calls out one of the following: Animal, fish, bird, person, something green, something with leaves, etc. The student who catches the paper wad must name something in that category while IT counts to five quickly. If the other student cannot respond in that time, he or she becomes IT.

❑ None

46. Break Out of Sin

Students stand in a circle, holding hands. Two or three sinners are chosen and stand inside circle. Sinners try to break out of the sin surrounding them. They cannot pull or bump into the arms of students in the circle. They may only escape by going under the arms of students.

Students who are forming the circle may not move feet. They can only keep sinners in by moving arms up and down.

❑ One inflated balloon (May want to have an extra balloon ready.)

47. Balloon Breakout

One student has a balloon and stands inside the circle of other students. Another student moves around the outside of circle. The circle may move arms and legs as needed to keep student from kicking a balloon outside the circle to hit that student. However, circle students must keep holding hands. They cannot touch the balloon with their hands.

If student on outside of circle is touched by the balloon, he becomes IT.

If student on inside of circle with balloon is not able to touch the outside student with the balloon after a short period of time, let another student take his place.

48. Alphabet Thanks

Students sit or stand in a circle. First one names something he is thankful for, beginning with the letter A. Next person must use B, etc. until all the letters of alphabet are used. You may want to give each person a limit of five seconds.

You can also make this more difficult by having each person say the name and the thing the person was thankful for for each person who came before. (Person number 26 must say all previous 25 names and things for each person.)

THINGS YOU'LL NEED...

❑ None

49. Quick Thinking

Identify the category(ies) being used. Then, students in a circle pass a paper wad as quickly as possible to the next student. When each student touches the paper, he or she must shout out words such as the following in the category chosen: *Consecutive words of the memory verse. Animals, birds, or fish. Names of the apostles. Ways to follow Jesus. At least 3 consecutive books of the Old or New Testament.*

THINGS YOU'LL NEED...

❑ One piece of scrap paper, wadded

50. Encouraging Words

Students form a circle. Each removes one shoe and places it inside the circle. One at a time, students go into circle, close eyes, and grab a shoe. They hold the shoe behind their back and say something kind and encouraging about the owner of the shoe. Then he holds the shoe out in front of him, and the owner of the shoe steps forward and says something encouraging to the person holding his shoe.

Since children do not know who owns the shoe, this helps children say kind things about people they don't know.

THINGS YOU'LL NEED...

❑ None

❑ None

51. Guess Who?

Send one person out of the room.

Then, students choose someone to be the Roman Soldier (lost sheep, tax collector, fisherman, lion tamer, etc. to fit lesson). This person makes gestures and says phrases to drop hints to the guesser when he/she returns to the room. Other students answer normally.

Guesser comes back into room and asks questions such as: "Are you a man or woman?" "Do you fight in battles?" "Are you an animal that says, 'Baa'?" The guesser keeps asking until he finds out who is the Roman Soldier (or whatever the focus is for the lesson).

Repeat game with other people or items from lesson. Guesser asks questions to try to find out what person or object has been chosen and who is portraying it.

❑ Balloons
   (Games is better if all the balloons are the same color.)
❑ Small pieces of paper
❑ Pencils

52. Pop the Question

Give each student a balloon and a small piece of paper. (They may share pencils.) Have each one write down a question about the lesson. Then, have each student fold the paper into a small square and slip it into the balloon. Everyone blows up the balloons and ties them. (Some students will need help.) Place balloons in a corner of the room. On GO, students rush to get a balloon and pop it. (Step on it, sit on it, etc.) Then students read and answer the question in the balloon they popped.

❑ Paper
❑ Pencils

53. Witness

Use two or three students to help you stage a skit. (Pretend fight, car accident, bump into an old friend at the store.) Then, have students write down what they saw.

Stories will differ somewhat. Use this activity to show how the Bible was inspired by God. That is why several accounts of biblical history tell the same story.

54. David and Goliath

One student is Goliath. He stands at one end of the room. The rest of the group stands in a straight line on other side of room. The line of students are Davids. Each David has several pieces of wadded paper.

When Goliath turns his back, Davids pelt him with paper "stones" and move toward Goliath. Goliath quickly yells "Goliath" and turns to face the line of Davids. Davids stand still when they hear "Goliath." Anyone caught moving must start over. First to reach Goliath changes places with him for the next round.

THINGS YOU'LL NEED...

❑ Several paper wads

55. Sequence

Choose a subject. Each student in turn says one sentence about that subject. However, he must say what those in front of him said, then add his own sentence.

Sample:

Subject: Creation.

First person—God made the earth. Second—God made the earth. Then, He put the stars in the sky. Third—God made the earth. Then, He put the stars in the sky. He also made the sun to shine in the daytime.

(Classmates can help students remember when the list gets long.)

THINGS YOU'LL NEED...

❑ None

56. True Identity

IT is blindfolded. Classmates move in a circle around IT. When IT says, "STOP," circle stops moving. IT points to someone and asks, "Who are you?" That person says a name, not necessarily his own. IT decides if that is the true identity of the person. He has two guesses to find out who it is. If IT is right, that person becomes IT.

Use this game for one of these themes: Telling the truth. False teachers. Jesus knocks at door of our heart.

THINGS YOU'LL NEED...

❑ Blindfold

❏ Chalkboard
❏ Chalk
❏ Eraser
   or
❏ Whiteboard
❏ Marker

57. Blindfold Draw

On the chalkboard, have a student draw an item that corresponds with the lesson (church, pig, tree). Students take turns being blindfolded and trying to add an item to the drawing, such as: Bell on church, tail of pig, apple in tree.

❏ Blindfold
❏ Wad of paper for each student

58. Good Shepherd

Shepherd is blindfolded. His "sheep" are wads of paper, placed on the floor around shepherd's feet. All classmates are wolves. Wolves stand in a circle around the shepherd and his sheep. Wolves try to sneak up and capture a sheep (wad of paper from the floor).

If shepherd hears a noise, he points where he hears the noise. Then, he tries to guess who is sneaking toward him. (One or two guesses.) If correct, that wolf must sit out. Game is over when all wolves are out or all sheep have been captured.

If you have a large class, break the students up into groups of no more than 3-4 "wolves" each.

❏ None

59. Mt. Zion

IT stands at one end of the room and turns his back. While IT's back is turned, all classmates try to sneak forward and tag IT. When IT shouts, "Mt. Zion," he turns toward class. All classmates stop. If IT sees anyone moving, that person must go back and start over. Game is over when someone tags IT.

❏ One paper plate

60. Peer Pressure

Class stands in two lines, about three feet apart. One person is chosen to walk between the lines. This person wears an upside-down paper plate on top of head. The lines of students try to make plate fall off as person walks down the line. The only things they are allowed to do are to blow on the plate or fan their hands. They may not touch the person, move closer, or touch the plate.

61. Safety Zone

Three people are chosen to race through the "world" to the safety zone (a designated spot on other side of room). Other classmates are spaced around the room but cannot move from their spots.

The three racers wear upside-down paper plates on their heads. Classmates try to make enough breeze to cause plates to fall. Any racer that makes it to safety zone with the plate still on his head is a winner.

❑ Three paper plates

OUTDOOR FUN AT A MOMENT'S NOTICE

THINGS YOU'LL NEED...

❑ Plastic trash bag
❑ Yarn
❑ Net (trash can, chair, paper plates, yarn)

62. Giant Volleyball

Open a trash bag and swish to fill with air. Close quickly and tie with yarn. Play volleyball over any type of instant "net," such as a trash can, line of chairs from classroom, yarn tied to two trees, chairs, or poles, a line of paper plates on the ground.

THINGS YOU'LL NEED...

❑ None
Optional for alternative:
❑ Plastic trash bag, yarn

63. Moving Wickets

Form human wickets with two students who make a "bridge" with their arms. "Wickets" may move around designated playing area. Students try to run through the wickets. After a few minutes, allow other students to be wickets.

Alternative: Form two sets of human wickets and place one set at each end of playing area. Fill plastic trash bag with air and tie with yarn. Rest of students form into two teams and try to toss the "volleyball" trash bag through the opposing team's wicket. Wickets may move or not as you choose.

THINGS YOU'LL NEED...

❑ Choice of paper bags, yarn, plates, twigs, trash bag, paper, balloons, others as desired

64. Exaggerated Obstacle Course

Give students a few minutes to create their own obstacle course with some of the following items: Paper bags that students must step in and out of, yarn circle "lakes," paper plate paths that must be followed, pile of twigs that represent a mountain to be climbed over. Other "obstacles": Trash bag stuffed with papers or filled with air to jump over, balloons hung from a tree branch at different lengths. *(Students must duck under the balloons without touching them.)* Then, let the students run through their obstacle course. You may also add more activities such as: Leap frog, scissors walk, cartwheels in order to go through course. Or, run through once individually, second time in pairs, third time in triples, etc.

65. Centipede Stampede

THINGS YOU'LL NEED...

❏ None

Divide into two teams. Students hold waist of person in front. Teacher shouts how they will race: Hop two steps forward and one step back. Walk sideways. Walk three steps, stop and shout "Hallelujah!"

On GO, each team races to a goal following the command given. Each team must function as a team to get to the goal. If the line falls apart, it must go back to the beginning and start over.

66. Centipede Follow-the-Leader

THINGS YOU'LL NEED...

❏ None

Divide into three or more teams. Form centipedes as above. One team is the leader. Every team must follow and do what this team does. After a short time, choose another team to lead.

67. Life-Size Croquet

THINGS YOU'LL NEED...

❏ Three trash bags

Have pairs of students form wickets by facing each other and holding arms. All students except two or three will be wickets. Those students who are not wickets try to roll inflated trash bags (one bag for each child) through the moving wickets.

Give all students a turn at playing this giant croquet. If you have a large group, half of the students can be wickets and the other half croquet players.

- ❏ Four paper plates
- ❏ Stapler
- ❏ A few balloons (or paper wads)

68. Paddle Baseball

Your students will enjoy playing this wacky version of baseball. Before going outside, make one or two paddle-bats by stapling two plates together (insides together to form a pocket). Leave about four inches open for students to fit a hand into. You can cut it a bit to make the "mitt" more comfortable.

Also, take a few balloons to blow up outside. (If it's a windy day, crumple up a piece of scrap paper to use as a ball.)

Once outside, change the normal rules of baseball by having more than three bases, making the students run backward from base to base, or make the runner hit a ball at each base.

- ❏ Two or more paper plates
- ❏ Stapler
- ❏ Yarn

69. Plate Soccer

Make one or more soccer-plates by stapling two plates together (insides together as above). Let the students play this modified version of soccer. Goals can be yarn circles.

Designate two goals, one directly opposite the other, with plenty of playing area between. Each of the two teams choose a goalie who tries to keep plates from entering the goal area.

Teams begin to play in middle of playing area. Each team tries to kick the plates down the field and into the goal of opponent. (You may want to have extra soccer-plates in case the original one gets destroyed from being kicked.)

- ❏ Two or more paper plates
- ❏ Stapler
- ❏ Yarn
- ❏ Newspaper (optional)

70. Plate Hockey

Use the same concept as above. Make hockey sticks from rolled up newspaper or paper plate paddles.

Make one or two "pucks" using same directions as soccer-plates. You may want to make them with the smaller dessert paper plates. Also, make a paddle-bat for each player, or use rolled up newspaper. Play this hockey game with same directions as soccer, except "puck" is moved with paddle-bats or rolled up newspaper for hockey sticks.

71. Plate Frisbees

❑ 6–10 paper plates
❑ Stapler

Make a frisbee for groups of about five students to play with. Staple two plates together (insides together to form a pocket). You may make more if you have plenty of plates. Toss frisbees around for as much time as you have.

Alternative: **Frisbee golf** can be played by placing obstacles on the ground such as a square formed by twigs or yarn circles. (Make squares or circles about 2 feet across.) Number each "hole." Students must toss frisbee into each "hole" in order. Make the course as difficult or as easy as you wish. Students may play in teams or individually.

OUTDOOR GAMES WITH BIBLE THEMES

72. Fish Net

THINGS YOU'LL NEED...

❑ None

Depending on size of group, choose one or more sets of three students to be fish nets. Other students are fish. Game is played within pre-established boundaries. Fish "net" group must hold hands and move in a line to try to surround a "fish" (student). Students on ends of fish "nets" clasp hands to complete a circle around the fish to capture him.

Use this game to reinforce lesson about Jonah, fishers of men, or the great catch of fish.

73. Battle Tag

THINGS YOU'LL NEED...

❑ None

Designate 1-3 soldiers. Soldiers chase other students and tag them. Students must hold the spot where they were tagged, such as grabbing shoulder, holding onto ankle, clutching heart.

Soldiers may only tag a student once each time he touches him. When a student cannot hold another spot, stand or move, he must sit out. Continue game until many students are out, then start over with different soldiers.

Use game with any lesson about battles or soldiers from the Old or New Testament.

74. Come-Along Tag

Begin a game of tag with one IT. Each time IT tags someone, that person must join hands or link arms with IT, but only IT can tag another student. Play until most of the group has joined IT.

75. Freedom

Choose one Judge. The rest of the group are all "guilty." The guilty persons may stand in a line or sit on the ground. The Judge calls each guilty person forward, one at a time. Judge gives "guilty" a way to gain freedom, such as spell Methuselah then do a cartwheel; name 12 apostles and run around the group backward; tell the order of creation and go find a twig; say the first and last word of the Bible and skip to the door and back, etc. (Several guilty persons may be completing their feats at once.)

76. Room at the Inn

Choose four "inns." (Tree, corner of building, picnic table, one square on sidewalk, etc.) Students divide up and stand at any "inn" that they choose. IT stands in the middle of playing area and asks for a room. All students shout, "No Room!" Then, IT says, "TRAVEL!" Everyone at all the inns must TRAVEL to another inn. IT tries to tag someone as they are running. The tagged person becomes IT.

Play this game to reinforce the story of Jesus' birth or the Good Samaritan.

77. Selfish Animals

Designate playing area. Students move around, pretending to be the animals that you name. *i.e. Monkeys, kangaroos, frogs, etc.* While moving, students try to tag the others and make them lose their animal position. Any who do not keep the animal position are out.

❏ None

5 GAMES TO MAKE AND PLAY

❑ Paper plates
❑ Sheets of paper or large pieces of newsprint
❑ Crayons

78. Answer Boards

Give each student a paper plate and a sheet of paper or a large piece of newsprint. Also, give each one a crayon.

Allow a short time for students to design a game board with nine, twelve, or more squares. They should all have the same number of spaces to fill up. (They can make pie shapes on the plates, if desired.)

Ask questions about the lesson, or quiz them on books of the Bible, names of apostles, the Ten Commandments, or order of creation, etc. The first student to raise his hand answers. A correct answer allows that student to fill in one space on his board. If the answer is wrong, let all students write down their answers on a separate piece of paper. Every student who writes the right answer fills in a square on their game board.

Students may fill in their squares however they wish. First one with a full board wins. (Or, a straight line, an X, or whatever you say ahead of time.)

THINGS YOU'LL NEED...

❑ Ball of yarn for each team

79. Follow Jesus on the Narrow Path

Give one team a short time to construct a maze with yarn for the other team to follow. They can string the yarn around things in the room or in an outside area. The other team follows the maze, picking up the yarn as they go. They must backtrack if they get to a place where the yarn is overlapped by other yarn.

If you have a large space, let each team make a separate maze for the other to follow. (Don't let the two overlap.)

80. Funny Feet/Hands Relay

Each team makes one pair of feet by stapling two plates together for each foot. Cut a small horseshoe shape on top to fit the foot into. Then, have them cut four oversized hand-shapes from either a paper plate or construction paper and staple together to make one pair of big gloves.

For the relay, each member of the team takes a turn doing the following: Put on the shoes and walk to a table. Pick up their team's "glove" and put it on their hands. Then they walk to the chalkboard, pick up the chalk with the hand in the "glove," and make an X on the board.

They then put the chalk down, go to the table, and take off hands. Then they may run or walk in their "shoes" back to their line and take shoes off for the next person to use. Continue until all members have had a turn. If the shoes or gloves fall apart, team must put it back together before continuing.

HINT: If you have a slippery floor, you may want to just use the hands.

81. It's in the Tube

Each of two or more teams uses newsprint to make paper tubes. Each tube must be at least six feet long. They may need to tape several smaller tubes together.

The first team to construct a six-foot tube, hold it over their heads, and roll a paper wad through it, wins.

Alternative: For even more fun, tape 2-foot sections of tubes together at different angles and see how far students can get paper wad while holding this giant paper maze over their heads.

THINGS YOU'LL NEED...

❑ Paper for each student
❑ Pencils
❑ Paper bag

82. Know Your Church Treasure Hunt

Give each student a small piece of paper and a pencil. Everyone thinks of one clue about their church building and writes it down.

Encourage them to avoid places that have classes going on at this time, such as nurseries or other classrooms.

Some suggestions: I contain more letters than you can count. (Library.) Fa La La. (Choir loft.) I make a clean sweep. (Janitor's closet.)

Then, fold all the clues and place them in a paper bag. Divide the class into two teams. Each team alternates drawing clues out of the bag until each team has half. Teams then must figure out what the clue means, go to each place, and be prepared to tell something about it. (Library has new red carpeting. Janitor's closet door is locked.)

You may need a helper, so that both teams are escorted by an adult.

THINGS YOU'LL NEED...

❑ Paper plates
❑ Yarn
❑ Balloons

83. Hop-Skip

Each student cuts the center from a paper plate and ties a 3-foot length of yarn to the rim. Then, have each child blow up a balloon and tie it to the yarn. Students slip foot through the plate rim.

Now, they try to swing the plate with their ankle, making the balloon spin around. They must hop over yarn and balloon while spinning it with their ankle. Play until balloons are broken.

THINGS YOU'LL NEED...

❑ Paper
❑ Yarn
❑ Scissors
❑ Straws

84. Butterfly Race

Each pair of students folds a piece of paper and cuts a backward C, leaving the back of the C on the fold. Unfold this shape to make butterfly wings. Tape a straw on the fold.

Next, have each pair cut a long length of yarn. Slip yarn through the straw. Pairs race their butterflies with other pairs by holding the yarn tight and letting straw slide across the yarn.

Winners of each race compete until a final winner is declared.

Lesson in this game is cooperation. Student on each end of yarn will have to cooperate with partner to help win.

85. Name Game

THINGS YOU'LL NEED...

❑ Paper
❑ Pencils
❑ Paper bag

This game is played like Bingo. Students create their own cards by writing an assigned name across top of paper. (Teacher tells students which name from Bible to use. For example: Abraham, Deborah, Joseph.)

Students draw a line down paper to separate each letter. Then, draw lines across the page to make squares. Have about four squares down, but number of squares across will depend on name used.

Teacher gives clues about the person, writing them down on small pieces of paper as they are given. Students write the clues in their squares in any order they choose.

Teacher then puts each of the papers in a paper bag or other container, draws out one at a time, and reads it. Students mark an X on the clues as they are read. (Or, use small bits of paper to cover the clues so cards can be used more than once.)

First person to get a line covered either across or down wins.

86. Paper Bag Targets

THINGS YOU'LL NEED...

❑ Paper bag for each student
❑ Scissors
❑ Crayons
❑ Scrap paper to wad up

Each student makes a target by cutting a medium-sized hole in one side of a paper bag. He then colors that side of the bag, using the hole as part of a picture. (For instance: a person with a big mouth, a wishing well, etc.)

When all targets are finished, line them up against a wall. Give each student a piece of paper to wad up. Students take turns trying to get paper wad through hole of target.

87. Match-Pic

Divide into two teams. Students make and play a game similar to the one above. However, one team writes a word on each square, and the other draws a simple picture to match the word. (Have each team do 5 words and 5 pictures to save time.)

Play game as above, matching words with corresponding pictures.

88. True/False

Divide into two or more teams. Each team tears paper into eight or ten squares. Teams use Bibles or concordances to find an interesting Bible fact to write on each square. They write some real facts and some which are not. (i.e. Balaam was a talking donkey. False. Balaam owned a donkey that talked.) Be sure to have them write whether the fact is true or false on their card, in case they forget when reading them to the others.

When each team has finished making their cards, they take turns reading their cards to the other teams. Other teams try to guess whether the facts are true or false.

If you choose to keep score, the team that fools the others the most times wins.

89. Match Game

Divide into two teams. Each team tears a piece of paper into the same number of squares (one or more for each student).

Students write a word that corresponds with the lesson on one square of paper (star, sheep, shepherd, manger, Mary, etc.). Each team will make a set of words exactly like the other team's set. Both teams place squares of paper, face down, on a table or the floor. Mix up the squares so picking mates will be more difficult.

First member of one team chooses two squares. If they match, team keeps squares. If there is no match, member places them back where he got them, face down. Then, first member of the other team chooses.

Game ends when all squares are gone. Team that has the most squares wins.

90. Paper Plate Tic-Tac-Toe

Give each student a paper plate. He draws a tic-tac-toe board in the center of it (nine squares).

Then, each student makes ten playing pieces of their choice, five of one kind and five of another. Playing pieces can be plain circles, squares, or students may color on the pieces to make animals, objects, or people that correspond with current lesson theme.

Students pair up and play tic-tac-toe.

THINGS YOU'LL NEED...

❑ Paper plate for each student
❑ Crayons
❑ Scissors
❑ Construction paper

6 CREATIVE WAYS TO REVIEW LESSONS AND TRUTH

TEAMS

❑ Paper
❑ Pencils
❑ Tape

91. Bible Verse Shenanigans

Each member of team writes a designated part of a memory verse on a piece of paper. Each team member tapes his piece of paper to the back of knees, ear, elbow, shoulder, or whatever. Team then stands in line to displays the verse. Class reads it outloud.

Alternative: Other team must move the members of the first team into the right order to read the verse by calling out, "Elbow first. Shoulder stands next to elbow, etc."

❑ Paper
❑ Pencils
   or
❑ Chalkboard
❑ Chalk

92. Acrostic

Each team is given one key word or person from the lesson. They may work at the chalkboard or use paper and pencils. Write the key word vertically. Students use those letters as any letter of a word related to that topic or person.

When all are finished, have the teams show their acrostics to the class.

For example:

```
    G o D
    p r a y
    d e n
D a r i u s
    r e s c u e d
    l i o n s
```

40

Alternatives: Students can make a Cross-Word puzzle (puzzle in the shape of a cross) using any words from the lesson. Or, students may choose to make an X puzzle instead.

```
    N       h
     i     a
      n
       o  e
    J     v
           e
            h
```

Students review the lesson content while making up the puzzles.

93. Bible Verse Mix-Up

THINGS YOU'LL NEED...

❑ Paper
❑ Pencils

Each team writes out the designated verse with one or more words on each piece of paper, depending on how large the teams are. The team mixes up the verse and stands in front of class. However, they leave out one word of the verse (or more). Class is given 10 seconds to discover which word(s) is missing. Repeat for all teams.

94. Roving Reporter

THINGS YOU'LL NEED...

❑ Paper
❑ Pencils

Have each team develop a funny reporter character and choose who he or she will interview. They may talk about a character in the lesson or focus on imaginary witnesses to a biblical event. Allow them time to write down the interview and practice the skit. Then have each team present their interviews to the class.

Topic Ideas: Our church. Why our class loves Jesus. Ways we follow our Lord, etc.

Alternatives: Taped Interviews. You will need a tape recorder/player and blank tape. Allow one team to tape this week and another next week, depending on time allowed. Students can do the activity as a whole group if desired.

- ❏ Old magazines
- ❏ Paper
- ❏ Scissors
- ❏ Glue
- ❏ Crayons or colored markers
- ❏ Pencils

95. Memory Verse Rebus Puzzle

Teacher writes a verse on the chalkboard so all teams can see it. Students think of word pictures to substitute for the words of the verse. Then they cut out and glue pictures, letters, numbers, etc. from the magazines to write the verse as a rebus. They can also write numbers and letters or draw pictures and shapes.

Example: For (4) God (picture of gold - L) so (needle and thread) loved (heart)....Other word suggestions: GR8 = great, B4 = before, N = in.

- ❏ Old magazines
- ❏ Paper
- ❏ Scissors
- ❏ Glue
- ❏ Crayons or colored markers

96. Write a Rebus Story

Students cut out pictures from magazines and use them to re-tell a Bible story in a rebus story. They can also choose to draw some of the pictures.

Example: God told Noah (picture of old man instead of the word "Noah") to build an ark (picture of boat instead of word "ark") and fill it with animals (pictures of animals, preferably in pairs). A rebus story reads easier if each of the picture words are used several times.

This can be used to reinforce any Bible lesson.

- ❏ Paper or newsprint
- ❏ Crayons or colored markers
- ❏ Pencils

97. Design an Ad

Give the groups 5-10 minutes to create an ad that will convince others to do one of the following: Follow Jesus. Want to attend your church. Want to live in their family. Stay away from sin. Anything that reinforces the current lesson truth or theme.

Students draw or write the ad on paper or large sections of newsprint. Then present them to the class. If possible, you may want to have them present their ads to an adult Sunday School class or the congregation in a special presentation. If you have some that are really good, see if they can be reproduced in the church bulletin.

98. Write a Word-Picture Story

THINGS YOU'LL NEED...

❑ Old magazines
❑ Paper
❑ Scissors
❑ Glue
❑ Crayons or colored markers

Using the same concept as the Bible Rebus Story above, have the students write a modern story that relates to the day's lesson theme or truth (keeping a promise; living for Jesus, obeying parents, telling the truth).

This will help the students make their own life-related application of the Bible story.

99. Television/Radio

THINGS YOU'LL NEED...

❑ Paper
❑ Pencils

Encourage creativity by giving students the opportunity to write a radio or television program based on the lesson. Give them several minutes to develop it. Then, have them present their creations today or save them for next week, depending on time, or use them in a church presentation.

100. Crushed Idols

THINGS YOU'LL NEED...

❑ Paper bags
❑ Crayons or colored markers

Give each team a paper bag and crayons or colored markers. Have them write on the bag: Things they love like bike, stereo, leather jacket, money. Places they spend time like an arcade, ball games, Disneyland. Things they like to do like watch TV, use a computer, go fishing. Or have them list some of their heroes.

After a few minutes, have each team stand their bag up in front of the class and tell about these things.

Then, tell the class that these are the things that we allow to become our idols. While it's okay to enjoy the things around us, God should always come first.

Ask the class to tell ways the things they have listed can become idols. (Go to ball games instead of church. Spend my money on these things instead of sharing with those in need or giving an offering at church.)

Then have the teams stomp on their idols to crush them.

101. Fun Story

THINGS YOU'LL NEED...

❑ None

You can review any lesson by re-telling the story this way.

Instruct students to listen for certain words in the story. You may want to list them on the chalkboard to help them remember. Then have them do certain actions each time they hear those words.

Example:

Cross = stand up and hold arms out to sides, so you look like a cross. Jesus = Touch palms where nail scars would be. Sea = Make waves with your arms.

102. Room Full of Blessings

THINGS YOU'LL NEED...

❑ Paper bags
❑ Crayons or colored markers
❑ Magazine pages or newsprint for stuffing

Students color the front of a paper bag to look like themselves. On the back and sides of the bag, they write ways that they can be a blessing to others.

When finished, have them stuff their bags loosely with magazine pages or newsprint. Tape or staple the bags closed and place blessings all around the room.

103. Progressive Mural

THINGS YOU'LL NEED...

❑ One long piece of newsprint
❑ Crayons or colored markers
❑ Timer, optional

Roll out a long strip of newsprint and give each student a 2 feet x 2 feet section. (Keep long strip intact.) Students write at the top of their section one person, item, or scene from the day's lesson.

Then, have the students move over one position and begin drawing the item named underneath the word(s). After a minute or two, have the students move down the line again and work on next item. (Ones on end come around to other end and fill that space each time students switch.) Keep progressing until the mural is complete.

If you wish, use a timer and have children switch positions at the sound of the bell or buzzer.

104. Tent Living

Have students make a replica of the Israelites' tent city in the wilderness. Encourage them to be realistic by showing outdoors cooking, wells, sheep pens, etc. that any of the Old Testament characters (Abraham, Moses, Jacob, etc.) would have lived in.

THINGS YOU'LL NEED...

- ❑ Bibles
- ❑ Newsprint or other paper
- ❑ Pencils
- ❑ Crayons or colored markers
- ❑ Scissors
- ❑ Glue
- ❑ Tape
- ❑ Straws

105. God's Champions

Make a poster from newsprint and title it: God's Champions. Each student will name something that he or she is a champion at — Bible reader. Gymnastics winner. Fast runner. Eating a double-decker ice cream cone without spilling a drop. (Help each student think of things that they may not consider. Anything counts!)

Each child in your class has special qualities. Encourage them to look for ways God has made them special for Him. Be prepared by coming to class with at least one idea for each child if they cannot think of one. This will also let them know that you think they are special.

THINGS YOU'LL NEED...

- ❑ Newsprint
- ❑ Crayons or colored markers

106. Our World Records

Give the class the opportunity to make a book with their own "world" records in it. Ideas might be: Jim jumped up and down 100 times while saying his memory verse. Adam drank 12 glasses of punch at our last class party. Rachel can fit 300 braids in her hair. Anything goes, as long as it builds and encourages the students with a little humor.

THINGS YOU'LL NEED...

- ❑ Several sheets of paper
- ❑ Pencils
- ❑ Stapler

45

❏ Bibles
❏ Newsprint or other paper
❏ Pencils
❏ Crayons or colored markers
❏ Scissors
❏ Glue
❏ Tape
❏ Straws

107. Tabernacle/Temple

This can be a spur-of-the-moment activity, but it will take extra minutes of several class times to complete. Have the students get out newsprint, pencils or crayons, scissors, glue, tape, straws, and Bibles. Once students get started on this project, they leave materials out, if possible, or place pieces in a paper bag until ready to put whole item together.

Students can use Exodus 26 to find how to build a tabernacle, and I Kings 6—7 for a temple.

Scale all buildings to the height of a straw or a half-straw. Measurements need not be exact.

The students will learn a lot by making their own versions of these Old Testament places of worship. If desired, have half the class do a temple and the other half do a tabernacle, or have all just work on one.

❏ Bibles
❏ Newsprint or other paper
❏ Pencils
❏ Crayons or colored markers
❏ Scissors
❏ Glue
❏ Tape

108. Palace Living

The castles of any of the kings and queens of Israel and Judah are always fun for students to make. They can use their Bibles for research or just use their imaginations. Groups or the whole class can work on a palace. (See I Chronicles 14:1; II Samuel 11:2 for Solomon's, David's, or Saul's palaces.)

109. Cartoon Lesson

Assign each student or pair of students one scene from the lesson. Each draws and colors a cartoon scene which reflects the lesson, the characters, or the Bible truth. They may draw lines between scenes if desired. When finished, each student tells his part of the story.

ACTIVITIES FOR INDIVIDUALS OR PAIRS

110. Write a Psalm

Before you begin, you may want to review several of the psalms. Talk about what each one does. Does it offer praise or worship? Is the writer asking for help? Tell students to use the book of Psalms as a guideline. Let them know that their psalm can praise God, ask for help, or tell how God has taken care of them. The length is not important.

THINGS YOU'LL NEED...

❑ Bibles
❑ Paper
❑ Pencils

111. Write a Proverb

Proverbs are wise sayings. They express truths in very short sentences, often by comparison and contrast. Have the students use the book of Proverbs as their guide and make up two or more Proverbs. Suggest some topics, such as getting along as friends, how to cope in today's world, ways God expects us to act.

THINGS YOU'LL NEED...

❑ Bibles
❑ Paper
❑ Pencils

112. Write a Prayer

Patterned after the Lord's Prayer (Matthew 6:9-13) or a psalm, have the students write a prayer that would be to God from people today.

THINGS YOU'LL NEED...

❑ Paper
❑ Pencils
❑ Bibles

113. Draw a Proverb

Have students select a Proverb and draw a picture to illustrate it. Example: Holding your tongue (10:19b), a mouthful of gravel (20:17), eating too much honey and getting a tummy ache (25:16).

THINGS YOU'LL NEED...

❑ Bibles
❑ Paper
❑ Crayons

❑ Paper
❑ Crayons

114. Cartoon Lesson

Students draw a cartoon strip which tells about a time when they needed forgiveness or needed to forgive someone else. When they helped someone or needed God's help. Told someone about Jesus or received Jesus as Savior, etc. (Anything to correspond the day's lesson or a quarterly theme.)

Students may show their drawings to the class, or you may put them all on a bulletin board.

Alternative: If you have the computer, scanner, and printer capability, put them together into a cartoon booklet and give one to each student.

❑ Paper
❑ Pencils
❑ Crayons or colored markers

115. In Crowd

Discuss cliques with the students. A good explanation is a group that only allows certain people to be their friends. A clique often hurts the feelings of others and people in them often act as though they are better than others.

Establish your class as a non-clique. Call it the "In Crowd." The only rules in this group will be:
1. We include anyone who comes to class.
2. We do our best to act like Jesus.

Draw up a class pact that says this group will not exclude anyone from our "in crowd," and that each member will do his/her best to act like Jesus. Have everyone sign it.

Then have students design a logo to represent the group. Be sure all the students help design the logo. Use symbols that represent togetherness, Jesus, love, etc. Each student should participate in drawing or coloring a part of the logo. When finished, hang it up in the classroom.

❑ Paper
❑ Pencils
❑ Crayons or colored markers

116. Continuous Verses

Have students cut out a shape to match the memory verse, lesson content, or lesson truth. They may color the shape. Then, have them write a continuous verse around the edge. For example, the world or a house with John 3:16 or Joshua 24:15c written around the outside edge.

117. Narrow Vision

Have one student put his hands at each side of his face, like blinders, or wear the paper blinder. The rest of the class stands on each side of this person and does actions (holding arm as if hurt, laying on floor begging for food, takes off shoes as if does not have any, two have a pretend fight, etc.). Person with blinders tries to guess what is going on.

Discuss how we need to be alert so we can see what goes on around us, not ignoring areas in which we can help. Talk about what kinds of blinders we sometimes have that keep us from seeing the needs of others.

THINGS YOU'LL NEED...

- ❏ None or you can make a paper blinder from two pieces of construction paper and a strip of paper about 2 inches wide. Attach the strip of paper to the back of the construction paper sheets so it drapes over the head and stays there with most of the paper toward the face, extending beyond the eyes.

118. Lips Booklet

On a piece of folded paper (fold is at the bottom of lips), the student draws a freehand outline of lips and cuts it out. Then, color the lips and write one of the following or another verse which the student selects.

Outside	Inside
Psalm 119:13	Write out the verse.
Exodus 20:1-17	Write one of the 10 Commandments.
Job 27:4	Write out the verse.
Psalm 19:14	Write out the verse.

THINGS YOU'LL NEED...

- ❏ Bibles
- ❏ Paper
- ❏ Pencils
- ❏ Crayons or colored markers
- ❏ Scissors

119. Heart Booklet

Students cut a heart shape from a piece of folded paper. Be sure the fold is on the left side.

Outside	Inside
Psalm 28:7	Write out the verse.
Psalm 119:11	Write out the verse.
I John 3:20b	Write out the verse.

Or, have the students use the concordance in their Bibles to find other verses which talk about the words heart and love.

THINGS YOU'LL NEED...

- ❏ Bibles
- ❏ Paper
- ❏ Pencils
- ❏ Crayons or colored markers
- ❏ Scissors

Students may also draw a picture of how to show love, how God shows love to him, etc. If desired, make more than one folded heart and put together into a multi-paged booklet.

THINGS YOU'LL NEED...

❑ Bibles
❑ Paper
❑ Pencils
❑ Crayons or colored markers
❑ Scissors

120. Follow

Using the same concept as above, have students draw a foot shape by tracing their own foot and cut it out of folded paper so that the fold connects the heel. Have them write any of the following or something else they choose.

Outside	Inside
Followers of Jesus	12 apostles/Matthew 10:2-4
Matthew 16:24	Write out verse.
I Corinthians 14:1a	Follow the way of love.
I Peter 2:21	Follow in Jesus' steps.

THINGS YOU'LL NEED...

❑ Bibles
❑ Paper
❑ Pencils
❑ Crayons or colored markers
❑ Scissors

121. Light

Make a light bulb shape with the fold at the left side. Encourage students to write any of the following or ways they can be a light for Jesus at home or school.

Outside	Inside
Genesis 1:3	Write out the verse.
Matthew 5:14a	You are the light of the world.
John 1:3-4	Write out the verses.
I John 1:5b	Write out the verse.

THINGS YOU'LL NEED...

❑ Bibles
❑ Paper
❑ Pencils
❑ Crayons or colored markers
❑ Scissors

122. Beatitudes

Make a large smiling face with the fold on the left. Label the outside: My Be-Happy Attitudes. Inside have students write out the beatitudes found in Matthew 5:3-12 on the left hand side. Then on the right hand side, have them write each verse in contemporary language that applies to their lives. For example (verse 4), "If I am sad, Jesus will comfort me."

123. Handprints

THINGS YOU'LL NEED...

❑ Bibles
❑ Paper
❑ Pencils
❑ Crayons or colored markers
❑ Scissors

Make handprints with one edge on the fold. Encourage students to write any of the following or ways they can use their hands to serve Jesus. Or, make them praying hands to emphasize people and situations they need to pray for.

Outside	Inside
Luke 22:40b	Help me not to give in to temptation.
I Corinthians 10:13	Write out verse.
Hebrews 4:16	Write out verse.
Isaiah 50:9a	It is the Sovereign Lord who helps me.
Psalm 24:4	Lord, help me to have clean hands and a pure heart.
Psalm 90:17	May everything my hands do bring honor, Lord, to you.
Acts 20:34	Let my hands serve others.

124. Patience Game

THINGS YOU'LL NEED...

❑ Paper
❑ Crayons or colored markers

Help students learn to be patient with themselves or with others who have handicaps.

Instruct students to: Write their name with their opposite hand. Write with their toes. Write with the blunt end of a crayon. Put a piece of paper on top of the head, and draw a face. Close their eyes and write out today's memory verse.

CREATIVE WAYS TO USE CURRICULUM

❑ Pieces of old or outdated curriculum
❑ Paper
❑ Glue
❑ Pencils
❑ Bible

125. Make Up a Parable

Let each student choose a picture to glue onto paper. Then, have each student write a parable to go with it. A parable is an earthly story with a heavenly meaning. If your lesson did not focus on a parable, you may wish to have the students review one or two from the Bible. *(Matthew 7:24-27, Wise and foolish builders; Matthew 13:1-8 and 18-23, The sower and the seed; Matthew 18:12-14, Lost sheep.)*

❑ Pieces of old curriculum
❑ Paper
❑ Glue
❑ Scissors
❑ Yarn
❑ Paper plates
❑ Hangers (optional)

126. Mobiles

Each student chooses a Bible topic for his mobile. Items can be glued to other paper to make them more sturdy, then hung from edges of a paper plate. If you have hangers, those can be used instead of a paper plate.

❑ Pieces of old curriculum
❑ Paper
❑ Scissors
❑ Pencils
❑ Stapler

127. Bible Dictionary

Students can use pictures from used curriculum to make their own Bible dictionary. If you have enough materials, each can make his own. Or, make one dictionary to keep in classroom. Have students add to it each quarter or review it with each new class that comes into your grade.

128. Puppets

Your students can use the supplies listed to make a variety of puppets. They may use them to practice skits to perform for the class or to present to a younger class on another day.

Alternative: Cut the faces out of pictures and use them on paper bags to make hand puppets.

- ❑ Pieces of old or outdated curriculum
- ❑ Glue
- ❑ Tape
- ❑ Straws
- ❑ Paper bags
- ❑ Blank paper
- ❑ Scissors
- ❑ Paper bags (optional)

129. Charade Game

Students glue pictures to pieces of paper. The pictures can be anything from animals to Bible characters, nature items, Bible story scenes, and everyday activities. This game can be kept in the classroom to play.

To play charades, divide class into two or more teams. Lay all the game pictures face down on a table. One member of Team #1 chooses a picture randomly. He tries to get his team to say what is on the picture by acting, not talking.

These game cards can be kept in the classroom to play at other times, also.

- ❑ Pieces of old or outdated curriculum
- ❑ Glue
- ❑ Paper

130. Silly Legends

For fun, let the students choose a picture and write a legend. *Examples: The Legend of the Clumsy Camel.* (Based on the picture of a camel that traveled with Abraham, Noah, or even the Wise Men.) *The Happy Tree Branch.* (Based on a picture of where Zacchaeus sat to see Jesus.)

- ❑ Pieces of old or outdated curriculum
- ❑ Paper
- ❑ Glue
- ❑ Scissors
- ❑ Pencils

131. Creation Collage

Let students glue creation pictures to newsprint to make a poster or a banner. Encourage them to draw as they desire and write praises to God for His wonderful creation.

- ❑ Pieces of old curriculum
- ❑ Glue
- ❑ Paper
- ❑ Crayons or colored markers

❑ Pieces of old curriculum
❑ Glue
❑ Paper
❑ Crayons or colored markers

❑ Pieces of old or outdated curriculum
❑ Newsprint
❑ Glue
❑ Scissors
❑ Tape
❑ Crayons or colored markers
❑ Pencils

❑ Pieces of old or outdated curriculum
❑ Newsprint or posterboard
❑ Scissors
❑ Glue
❑ Tape
❑ Crayons or colored markers
❑ Pencils

❑ Pieces of old curriculum
❑ Newsprint
❑ Scissors
❑ Glue
❑ Tape
❑ Crayons or colored markers
❑ Pencils
❑ Old magazines

54

132. Bible Story Collage

Choose any Bible story and let the students make a poster or banner illustrating it.

133. Bible Heroes

Each student chooses a hero to focus on and makes a banner illustrating or stating what he likes about that person; why he or she is a hero.

Make the banner by using a long strip of newsprint and pictures from old curriculum. Students glue or tape the pictures onto newsprint and write what he likes about that person. Student may also choose to add drawings or pictures of how the person lived, etc.

134. I Was There Poster

Students make a poster of a favorite Bible story. They cut out pictures of the people involved in the story and glue onto large sheet of newsprint, construction paper, or posterboard.

However, they should cut the head off one of the character pictures and draw their own head. Some of the other characters may be the students' families and friends. Encourage them to write what it would have been like to be there.

135. Theme Posters

Have students work together on quarterly theme posters. They may use a group of old pictures of the Bible lessons on each poster. Depending on desired size, a poster can contain one story or a whole theme, such as the life of Joseph. It could be on the truths taught through the quarter with contemporary pictures reflecting how those truths can have personal, life application in their lives.

136. The Life Of...

Students work in groups to make books about the lives of Bible characters. For example, one group may focus on Paul. They glue pictures and stories of Paul from old materials onto pages for the book. They may also want to research in their Bibles for more information to add. The books will make great references for your classroom bookshelf.

THINGS YOU'LL NEED...

- ❑ Pieces of old or outdated curriculum
- ❑ Bibles
- ❑ Paper (plain or construction paper)
- ❑ stapler
- ❑ scissors
- ❑ glue
- ❑ tape
- ❑ crayons or colored markers
- ❑ pencils

137. Bulletin Boards

Give students free rein to design your classroom bulletin board. They may choose a Bible character, illustrate a psalm, or cleverly reproduce the lesson themes. They can staple pictures, lesson stories, and handwritten information onto the bulletin board.

THINGS YOU'LL NEED...

- ❑ Pieces of old or outdated curriculum
- ❑ Stapler
- ❑ Paper
- ❑ Crayons or colored markers
- ❑ Pencils
- ❑ Colored construction paper

138. Storybooks for the Preschool

Students can make Bible storybooks for your nursery and preschool classes. Have them make as many books as time allows. Glue pictures and lesson stories to pages and staple them together. Students may want to write the story beneath the pictures. They can also draw pictures and designs on a page for the book cover.

THINGS YOU'LL NEED...

- ❑ Pieces of old or outdated curriculum
- ❑ Paper
- ❑ Scissors
- ❑ Glue
- ❑ Crayons
- ❑ Stapler

139. Puzzles for the Preschool

Glue a large picture to a piece of construction paper for strength. Dribble glue around the outside edges and sprinkle glitter on the glue. Then, cut the picture apart into puzzle pieces.

An envelope for the puzzle pieces can be made by folding a piece of newsprint in half and stapling the sides. Leave top open. Write on the envelope what the puzzle picture is.

THINGS YOU'LL NEED...

- ❑ Pieces of old or outdated curriculum
- ❑ Construction paper
- ❑ Scissors
- ❑ Glue
- ❑ Glitter

THINGS YOU'LL NEED...

❑ Pieces of old or outdated
  curriculum
❑ Yarn
❑ Paper bags
❑ Paper
❑ Crayons
❑ Pencils

140. Mission Materials

Missionaries are always in need of lesson materials. Students can make storybooks for foreign or inner-city missions using any of the ideas in this chapter. They may also group together a story poster and matching activity pages for several lessons. Then, bundle together for mailing.

Your Pastor or Missions Chairperson will help you find a place to send the materials.

Add letters or pictures from the students to make a personal and encouraging package.

INSTANT ACTIVITIES TO ENCOURAGE AND SERVE OTHERS

8

141. Servants

As the class arrives, number the students off in twos and set them apart in pairs. In the pairs, ones will be servants to twos for the first half of class. Then, switch places for last half so that the twos become the servants to the ones.

Servants pull chairs out for their partners, get pencils or whatever is needed for class, turn pages of Bibles and lesson books, etc.

Use this learning activity to reinforce serving one another, as when Jesus washed the disciples' feet and any lesson on serving others.

THINGS YOU'LL NEED...

❑ None

142. Encourage Your Friends

Students write their names on small slips of paper and put slips into a paper bag. One at a time, students pick a name out of the bag.

Give each student a piece of paper. They will make a friendship plaque for the person whose name they drew. On the plaques, they write the friend's name and follow it with encouraging words or a Scripture verse.

Example: David — Friend, Encourager, Prayer Warrior, Helper. Psalm 13:6.

Use to reinforce lessons on encouraging others as Jesus did and learning how to look for the good in others.

THINGS YOU'LL NEED...

❑ Paper
❑ Pencils
❑ Crayons or colored markers
❑ Glue
❑ 1 paper bag

- ❑ Paper
- ❑ Pencils
- ❑ Scissors

143. Gimme Five

Divide class into pairs. Each student traces and cuts out his handprint. Students put their partner's name on the handprint. Then they write five compliments or encouragements to each other. Give partners the handprints to take home.

Helps children learn how to build others up. Use to teach the meaning of the word "edify."

- ❑ Large piece of newsprint
- ❑ Crayons or colored markers
- ❑ Pencils

144. My Church Family Is Special

The class can work on a special mural for the entire church to enjoy. Students draw pictures, write poems or short stories, or express thanks to their church family. Remind students to include people such as: their families, the choir leader, preacher, janitor, secretary, and other people who make their church special. Display this special mural in the foyer or fellowship hall where all can enjoy.

Helps children learn why their church is special and why they are an important part of it.

- ❑ Paper
- ❑ Scissors
- ❑ Crayons or colored markers
- ❑ Pencils
- ❑ Bibles

145. Heart Promises

Make hearts of any size from paper. Students select and write a Bible promise on each heart. Promises can be some of the following: *Jesus loves you. God will see you through. I'm so glad you're here today. God hears your prayer.* Or, students can write out Bible verses such as Psalm 46:1-3, Psalm 18:2, Isaiah 46:11, Nahum 1:7, John 16:33, John 16:27, Philippians 4:7.

Dismiss class a few minutes early and have the students take the hearts with them to leave them in various places in the church—on pews, by the telephone, by the guest book, on Preacher's desk, in secretary's office, on someone's Bible.

Use as a learning activity to reinforces lessons on God's promises and how we can apply God's Word in our lives.

146. Thank You's

Students make thank you cards for anyone in the church family: Teens, Music Leaders, Nursery Workers, Bus Driver. Have them select and write out an appropriate verse on each card. Students deliver the thank you's after class.

Teaches or reinforces lessons on gratitude, thankfulness, why this is something God wants us to do.

147. Big Brother/Sister Encouragers

Let students choose to encourage a child from a younger class. Have each child determine which age level child he/she wants to be a big brother or sister to. Then have them write letters or make cards in class every now and then. Students do not have to know the child. Take students to the classes and meet their new "brother or sister" by choosing someone wearing the same color, someone with the same birthday, someone whose last name begins with the same letter as theirs, etc. (You may want to alert the other teachers that your class is going to do this.)

148. Encourage a Grandparent

Do the above activity, except write letters or draw pictures for an elderly person who attends church. The letters can be delivered in person after class.

If possible, find out about the older members of the church beforehand. Find out those who do not have grandchildren or do not have any living nearby. Have the child "adopt" this "grandparent" and do things for the "grandparent" throughout the quarter or the year.

❑ Paper and pencils for each group

149. Skits for Other Classes

Help students write and practice a skit to perform for another class. Writing and practicing may be done whenever you have a few extra minutes of class time. It may be a skit based on the Sunday Bible lesson or on a contemporary life-application truth derived from it. Students may work all together or in small groups.

Nursing home residents also will enjoy this activity if you take your class to one on a monthly or quarterly basis as a ministry outreach.

Alternative: Use old curriculum or paper bags to make puppets and use those to act out the skits students write. Younger children will love watching your class perform puppet plays for them. So will most nursing home residents.

❑ Paper
❑ Pencils
❑ Crayons or colored markers

150. Certificates of Appreciation

Students can learn to encourage others by making these certificates. They may write anything, such as: Great Friend; Bible Scholar; Prayer Warrior. Then, decorate the certificates and give them to classmates, parents, or other friends.

❑ Paper
❑ Crayons or colored markers
❑ Pencils
    Optional, after class
❑ Envelopes
❑ Stamps

151. Secret Pals

Teach children the joy of encouraging others without reward or credit. They will love the secrecy of this project. Let students write an encouraging letter or draw a picture. Don't have them put their names on the letters.

Mail the letters to business people of your church or some of the older members, leave them on the desks and in mail slots of church leaders; leave them in a bundle outside the door to another class.

Your class can do this activity several times during the year. Then, reveal the secret in the church bulletin or newsletter.

152. Shut-in Pen Pals

Have students write a letter to introduce themselves. If this is a last-minute project, get names of shut-ins after class. You may also take the letters to a local nursing home. This project can be done several times during the year.

Alternative: If desired, students can also draw pictures or cut them out of old curriculum pieces or magazines to tell a story about themselves that their "shut-in" neighbor can enjoy over and over.

❑ Paper
❑ Pencils

INSTANT ACTIVITIES FOR PRAYER AND WORSHIP

❑ Paper
❑ Pencils
❑ Scissors
❑ Crayons or colored markers

153. Prayer Coupons

Students cut small squares of paper, write coupons for prayer requests, and color them. The coupons promise to pray for someone each day this week.

Suggestions: To Preacher — This coupon good for 15 minutes of prayer for you and your family each day this week. I promise to pray for: (list specifics). To Our Janitor — this coupon good for 10 minutes of prayer for you and your family each morning and evening this week. I promise to pray for: (list specifics). To My Parents — This coupon is good for 15 minutes of prayer with you each day and 10 minutes of prayer for you every day. I promise to pray for: (list specifics) No expiration date.

❑ Paper
❑ Pencils
❑ Scissors
❑ Crayons or colored markers

154. Prayer Partners

Each student cuts out a medium-sized heart. Then cut the heart in half and have students write their name on both halves. Students exchange their heart halves with two other students. Instruct them to pray for those people each day this week.

Alternative: Put all of the paper heart halves in a large box, sack, or pile. Mix them up. Have students pull out any two and pray for those people each day this week.

155. Personal Prayer Journals

Students can make prayer journals by cutting a brown paper bag as a cover and decorating it. Or, they may use two pieces of construction paper, write: *Prayer Journal* on the outside, and decorate.

Staple several pieces of white paper inside the cover. Have students write at the top of each page: *Date, Prayer Request, Answer.* Encourage students to write in their prayer journals every day during the week. They can also add these columns: *Things God Taught Me Today* and *Blessings God Gave Me Today.* Encourage students to be thankful in prayer for those things, too.

Alternative: Provide old curriculum so students may glue a small picture on each page of their prayer books. They may want to add a prayer thought for each picture as they fill out their books.

THINGS YOU'LL NEED...

❑ Paper bags or construction paper
❑ Plain paper
❑ Staplers
❑ Pencils
❑ Crayons or colored markers

156. Class Prayer Journal

Take a few minutes of class time for the students to make a prayer journal as described above. Staple together a few pieces of paper inside two pieces of construction paper. Then, have students share prayer needs. Have one student write these needs in the book. Each week, pray for the needs, ask students to tell the class how God answered, and allow a short time for more needs to be entered into the journal. Be sure to have them record the prayer answers, so they can look back to see how God works in our lives.

Use as a learning activity to reinforce lessons on prayer.

THINGS YOU'LL NEED...

❑ Plain paper
❑ Stapler
❑ Pencils
❑ Construction paper
❑ Crayons or colored markers

157. Prayer Pal

Divide the students into pairs. Provide a short time each week for the prayer pals to pray together. (If students are absent, pair their partners up with someone else that week.)

THINGS YOU'LL NEED...

❑ None

Option: Have students record their Prayer Pal's request in their Prayer Journals and pray for them during the week.

158. My Hero

Have each student choose a Bible hero, a person they think did something special for God or someone they want to be like. They may work a short time each class period on this project (a poster or booklet). Using their Bibles and old curriculum pieces, have them write or draw several things about their hero. Include the things they admire most about this person, circumstances in which the person displayed his or her faith, how the student will try to be like that person in the Bible.

HINT: Heroes are important to children. They teach values and give them goals to strive for. This learning activity helps children recognize godly heroes and why they are important role models.

159. Reflect

If students haven't recently heard the story of the woman caught in adultery, review it quickly (John 8:3-11). Then focus on when Jesus knelt and began writing in the sand.

Tell the class that we don't know what Jesus wrote in the sand, but it made all of the woman's accusers slink away. Tell them to pretend that Jesus is in your room today, looking at them. If Jesus is writing the sins of each person present, what would He write about you? Students (and teacher) silently write on a piece of paper something that Jesus might write about them. Then, have personal, silent prayer asking Jesus to forgive that sin. Promise Him that you will try to do better this week.

When prayer is finished, have each student tear their paper up into tiny pieces and throw it away. Reassure each one present that that is what Jesus does with our sins when we confess them and tell Him we want to turn away from that sin. If appropriate and/or time allows, have three students read I John 1:9; Psalm 103:12; Romans 8:1 outloud.

160. Lessons to Live By

Let students staple some papers together into a book. They may cover and decorate it as desired. Each week, allow a few minutes at the end of class so students can write their own versions of the day's lesson and how it applies to their lives.

THINGS YOU'LL NEED...

❑ Paper bags
❑ Paper
❑ Stapler
❑ Pencils
❑ Crayons or colored markers

161. Prayer Circle

Have each student write his name on a small slip of paper. Pass the paper to person on the right. Instruct students to have a silent prayer for that person. If time, continue to pass papers to the right until papers reach the original person.

THINGS YOU'LL NEED...

❑ Small slips of paper
❑ Pencils

162. Prepare for Battle

Students help prepare their classmates for the coming week. Each student writes on a piece of paper one thing they will pray for to help each classmate through the week. *For example:* Good health. Pass that test at school. Help with a difficult situation.

Have the students tape these prayer promises to each person. Everyone should have one from each person in the class. They may wear the promises for the rest of class, if not inconvenient.

Alternative: Have students use their Bibles and concordances to look up a verse about prayer or God's help in trouble and include that verse as an encouragement to the person.

THINGS YOU'LL NEED...

❑ Paper
❑ Pencils
❑ Tape
❑ Bible (optional)

163. Share the Good News

Give students a few minutes to write or draw about something great that God did in their lives this past week. *(e.g.: Made Grandma well. Helped me when I felt sad. Gave my Dad a new job. Gave us sunshine for our game.)* Then, students can share their good news with the class. Have them tell how this encouraged their faith or what God may have taught them through it.

Alternative: Do the above activity. However, for a quicker activity, have students just tell their news.

164. Road Signs on the Narrow Path

Make road signs students can hang in their rooms to direct their daily walk with God. Students can freehand a sign (stop - octagonal/eight-sided, caution/warning sign - diamond, one way - rectangular information sign, etc.). Decorate as the student desires. They do not have to look like actual street signs.

Examples: STOP - yelling at my brother. One Way to Heaven.

If you have time, have students make signs which you can hang in the classroom to remind students to live for God each week.

165. Promise Book

Have students search in the Psalms for promises that are meaningful to them and offer help or encouragement in their daily lives. They may make a book of written promises, adding drawings as they wish.

Alternative: Make one to give away to someone else and a Promise Book of Encouragement. Students might want to make one to send to grandparents, aunts, uncles, friends, someone they've met at a nursing home, etc.

166. Wanted Poster

Students design a wanted poster with their picture drawn on it. They should write things they did this past week to glorify God. Poster is to show that this person is "Wanted by God for acting like a Christian."

THINGS YOU'LL NEED...

❑ Paper
❑ Pencils
❑ Crayons or colored markers

167. Sign Language

Make signs to show how Jesus guides our lives. Each student makes a sign that applies the truths of the day's Bible lesson to their daily lives in the coming week. Or have them work in pairs to make signs.

Examples: I worship at the feet of Jesus. Give all your worries to your Lord. I obey my parents because this pleases the Lord.

THINGS YOU'LL NEED...

❑ Paper
❑ Crayons or colored markers
❑ Pencils

168. Tell Someone About Jesus

Have students write a letter to someone who doesn't know Jesus. This letter won't be mailed, so encourage students to write just what they would say to this person about Jesus.

Encourage them to think about the people they know or meet this week and determine to tell at least one person why he or she needs Jesus as Savior.

THINGS YOU'LL NEED...

❑ Paper
❑ Pencils

169. Ode to God

Have students write a poem to tell God how much they love Him. Have volunteers read theirs when several are finished. Encourage those who do not finish before time runs out, to complete it at home and hang it where they can see it often.

Alternatives: Have students write a poem about *What the Cross Means to Me* or *Why Should I Worry When God Is on My Side.*

THINGS YOU'LL NEED...

❑ Paper
❑ Pencils

❏ Bibles
❏ Concordance
❏ Paper
❏ Pencils

170. Topic Focus

Students use their Bibles and a concordance to find out all they can about one topic. (Angels, Israel, Heaven, Sheep, Walking with the Lord, etc.) It may work better to have students work in groups. Students prepare a paper for presentation listing key attributes, benefits, purpose, etc.

The class may work on the same topic or give a different topic to each group.

❏ None

171. Mock Trial

Set up a courtroom and try to convict someone for being a Christian. Use evidence such as: He carries his Bible to school. I saw him helping an elderly person carry groceries.

INSTANT FUN WITH MUSIC

172. Musical Antics

One team performs a song for the other. The team should take a short time to make up a skit or song actions. No words can be used. Other team guesses which song is being performed.

Alternative: Team selects a song with which they are familiar from a song tape and acts it out while it is played.

THINGS YOU'LL NEED...

❑ Optional tape player and song tape

173. Instant Instruments

Let students use their imaginations to find instruments for their band. Some suggestions: Blow up and tie a balloon. Squeak the balloon with fingers. Blow up a balloon and do not tie. Let some air out with squeaky sounds. Put some crayons inside a paper bag to rattle. Tap the metal parts of two pairs scissors together. Tap two pencils together. Tap anything in the room (except classmates' heads) with pencils. Blow a little air into a paper bag and gather top closed. Hold top of bag and tap bag with pencil.

When everyone has chosen their musical instrument, select a familiar chorus and have the "band" provide the musical accompaniment. If you get good, try to perform the same chorus with "band" instruments for another class or the church congregation.

THINGS YOU'LL NEED...

❑ Crayons or colored markers
❑ Paper bags
❑ Scissors
❑ Pencils
❑ Other "musical" objects found in classroom
❑ Balloons

❑ None

174. Name the Tune

Divide the class into two teams. One team hums a few notes of a Christian song. Other team tries to guess what it is. First team may have to hum a little more. If second team guesses, they get to try to stump first team.

Alternative: Have other team decide in how many notes they can identify the song. If they do so, they get 10 points. If they don't, they must hum a tune for the other team who also decides in how many notes they can identify the song.

❑ Tape player
❑ Song tape

175. Follow the Choir Leader

Turn on a tape and let students take turns leading the group. Choir leader can act quite silly, have students do motions to songs, or not sing every other word, etc.

❑ Tape player
❑ Song tape

176. Laughing Song

Playing a tape on to keep students on track, have them laugh or giggle keeping time through a whole chorus.

❑ None

177. Cooperative Chorus

Students stand in a line or circle. Name a song. Using only the chorus, each student sings only one word, and so on until chorus is finished.

❑ None

178. Make a New Song

Divide class into 2 or more groups of students. Each group makes up a song using words or ideas from the day's lesson. Have each group choose a familiar tune to set their words to and sing it for the rest of the class.

179. Instrument-less Band

THINGS YOU'LL NEED...

❑ Optional tape player and song tape

Let students choose which part of the band they would like to be. Some suggestions are: Whistle, clap, tap feet, snap fingers, buzz lips. Play some familiar choruses with this interesting "band."

180. Castanet Band

THINGS YOU'LL NEED...

❑ Paper plates
❑ Stapler
❑ Old crayons
❑ Optional tape player and song tape

Each student folds a paper plate in half to make a castanet. Staple the sides, leaving a small opening. Drop a few old crayons into the opening and staple closed. Do some fun songs with your castanet band.

181. Silent Band

THINGS YOU'LL NEED...

❑ Tape player
❑ Song tape

This will be silly, but fun. Students choose a silent noise to do. Examples: Bat eyelashes. Wiggle ears. Open and close mouth like a fish. Twirl a pigtail. Flap arms. Have students form a circle so they can see each other and do their silent motions while a tape is playing a favorite song.

182. Sunday School Aerobics

THINGS YOU'LL NEED...

❑ Tape player
❑ Song tape

Let a student lead the group in aerobic exercises while a favorite song is playing. Have them use biblical moves, such as: Zacchaeus tree climbs, Noah water treads, Moses mountain climbing, fishermen net casting.

183. Memory Song

THINGS YOU'LL NEED...

❑ Paper
❑ Pencils

Have students form groups and select or make up a tune for the current memory verse. They may even make it into a rap song. After a few minutes, have the groups sing their songs to the class.

❏ Optional tape player and song tape

184. Chorus Fun

Use some familiar children's songs or the chorus to favorite hymns. Sing once through. Then, do the entire chorus with animal sounds (dogs, chicks, cats).

Alternative: Sing some favorite songs. On the chorus, clap for every other word.

❏ Paper
❏ Pencils
❏ Bibles (optional)

185. Bible Story Rap

Have students form groups of 2-4 people each. They choose a Bible story or use one that you assign them and make up a rap song that tells the story. Allow time to practice, then have them do their song for the class.

Index of Games
and
Learning Activities

ALPHABETICAL INDEX

The number given is the game number rather than the page number.
Games are numbered consecutively through the book.

BIBLE TRUTHS AND STORIES INDEX

The number given is the game number rather than the page number.
Games are numbered consecutively through the book.

GAMES AND LEARNING ACTIVITIES BY TYPE
INDEX

The number given is the game number rather than the page number.
Games are numbered consecutively through the book.

Chalkboard Games
   15, 24, 25, 30, 33, 35, 36, 37, 38, 57, 80

Circle Games/Activities
   1, 2, 3, 4, 5, 6, 9, 14, 18, 19, 43, 44, 45,
   46, 47, 48, 49, 50, 56, 58, 69, 71, 72,
   161, 177

Group Activities
   101, 102, 103, 104, 105 106, 107, 108,
   109

Ice-Breakers
   1, 2, 3, 4, 5, 6, 7, 8, 9, 10, 11, 12, 13,
   14, 15, 16, 17, 18, 19, 20, 21, 22

Lesson/Bible Verse Review
   23, 24, 26, 28, 29, 30, 31, 32, 33, 34,
   38, 39, 40, 43, 44, 49, 51, 52, 55, 56,
   57, 72, 73, 75, 78, 85, 88, 91, 92, 93,
   94, 95, 96, 97, 98, 99, 100, 101, 102,
   103, 104, 105, 106, 107, 108, 109, 110,
   111, 112, 113, 114, 115, 116, 117, 118,
   119, 120, 121, 122, 123, 124, 125, 126,
   127, 132, 133, 134, 135, 136, 158, 160,
   167, 170, 178, 185

Line Games/Activities
   7, 8, 9, 10, 14, 16, 18, 30, 31, 54, 60,
   65, 72, 80, 91, 103, 177

Memory Verse Activities
   30, 32, 43, 49, 91, 183

Mobiles
   126

Music
   172, 173, 174, 175, 176, 177, 178, 179,
   180, 181, 182, 183, 184, 185

Outdoor Games
   62, 63, 64, 65, 66, 67, 68, 69, 70, 71,
   72, 73, 74, 75, 76, 77

Pairs
   64, 67, 84, 110, 111, 112, 113, 114,
   115, 116, 117, 118, 119, 120, 121, 122,
   123, 124, 141, 143, 157, 167

Puppets
   128

Puzzles (picture)
   93, 139

Relays/Races
   14, 16, 20, 21, 22, 30, 39, 41, 42, 61,
   65, 80, 84

Skits
   53, 99, 149, 172

Teams/Groups
   1, 13, 14, 15, 17, 18, 20, 21, 22, 23, 24,
   25, 26, 27, 28, 29, 30, 31, 32, 33, 34,
   35, 36, 37, 38, 39, 40, 41, 42, 43, 54,
   58, 71, 72, 74, 75, 97, 98, 99, 101, 102,
   103, 104, 105, 106, 107, 108, 109, 115,
   136, 149, 170, 175, 178, 182, 183, 185